COURAGE

COURAGE

My Story of Persecution

FRESHTA TORI JAN

Norton Young Readers

An Imprint of W. W. Norton & Company
Celebrating a Century of Independent Publishing

To Agha Jan and Madar Jan—for your sacrifices.
To Ma and Poppy for giving me the childhood I missed.
To TJ, Tabasum, and Tim—my daily inspirations and
examples of resilience. To Rode and JP—you are missed
every day. And to all the world changers in the becoming.

<3

Series edited by Zainab Nasrati, Zoë Ruiz,
Amanda Uhle, and Dave Eggers.

Copyright © 2022 by The Hawkins Project and Freshta Tori Jan

Printed in the United States of America
First published as a Norton Young Readers paperback 2023

For information about permission to reproduce selections from this book, write to Permissions,
W. W. Norton & Company, Inc., 500 Fifth Avenue, New York, NY 10110

For information about special discounts for bulk purchases, please contact
W. W. Norton Special Sales at specialsales@wwnorton.com or 800-233-4830

Manufacturing by Lakeside Book Company
Book design by Hana Anouk Nakamura
Production manager: Beth Steidle

ISBN 978-1-324-05223-4 pbk.

W. W. Norton & Company, Inc., 500 Fifth Avenue, New York, N.Y. 10110
www.wwnorton.com

W. W. Norton & Company Ltd., 15 Carlisle Street, London W1D 3BS

0 9 8 7 6 5 4 3 2 1

CONTENTS

INTRODUCTION

Zainab Nasrati, Zoë Ruiz, and Dave Eggers

One of the best ways to understand a complicated moment in history is by reading the story of a person who lived through it. If you want to learn about what would drive a sixteen-year-old to fight for young women's rights to education in Burundi, reading her story will help you see the world through her eyes. This is what this series is all about: letting young people—who have seen and lived through recent world events—tell their stories.

It's important to understand other people's struggles, especially people who live in different places or come from different backgrounds than you do. Our hope with this book series is that by hearing one person's story, our readers will learn about many people's struggles and think about what we can do together to help make the world more peaceful and equitable.

Teenagers like Malala Yousafzai and Greta Thunberg became iconic for standing up for what they believe is right. Other teens, not yet as well known, have also stepped up to make a difference. When

Adama Bah was a teenager in post-9/11 New York, she was falsely accused of being a terrorist simply because she is Muslim. When Salvador Gómez-Colón was fifteen, his family endured Hurricane Maria in Puerto Rico. Using his deep local knowledge and incredible dedication to helping his neighbors, Salvador founded Light & Hope for Puerto Rico and raised money and gathered supplies to help islanders with basic needs during the emergency.

The I, Witness books will bring you stories of young people like you who have faced extraordinary challenges in their lives. Their stories are exciting and surprising, filled with struggle—and humor and joy, too.

We hope that you will consider your own life and your own story as you read. Is there a problem in the world or in your life that you would like to help solve?

In this book, you'll meet Freshta Tori Jan, who was born in Afghanistan as a member of a minority ethnic group. She faced discrimination and poverty as a young girl, and when she was twelve years old, threats from the Taliban—a ruling military organization that discriminates against women—forced her school to close permanently. In constant danger from the Taliban because of their ethnicity, her family had to fight for their safety, with someone in the house always staying awake all night to keep watch. Freshta helped her family survive by taking tutoring jobs teaching English. Her commitment to education helped them live, and it brought her new opportunities.

As a teenager, she was accepted into a high school in Texas and immigrated there on her own. There, she continued her education and founded an organization dedicated to helping others in need. We admire Freshta's empathy and her work to support people in need, and think that all of us can learn from what she faced and what she achieved. Some of us will never endure the terrifying things that she has, but all of us will do well to remember her strength and tenacity in the face of danger. Despite unthinkable challenges, Freshta approaches the world with kindness and generosity. As readers ourselves we were heartened and inspired by Freshta's story, and we hope you will be, too.

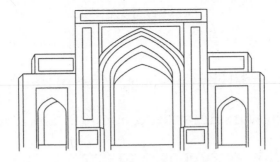

CHAPTER 1

Change

I was born in Herat, known as the poetic and artistic center of Afghanistan. In Herat, there are many historical buildings, and there are even artifacts that Alexander the Great left in the country around 300 BC.

My family and I lived in a house

surrounded by tall walls. Most of the families we knew in Herat lived behind walls like this, which were supposed to protect the women of the family and keep neighbors out of your business.

We had a big garden in our yard. We would all go out and dig up the soil and plant a whole variety of vegetables and fruits, like white and green onions, turnips, carrots, cucumbers, zucchini, and tomatoes. We also kept goats and sheep. As a toddler, I would sometimes ride the goats around the yard. I was so small they looked like horses to me. We also had a dog, Gorgi, that I loved with all my heart.

At night, I loved looking up at the stars in the yard.

When I was four years old, I was outside one night looking at some of the most beautiful stars I'd ever seen. Suddenly I saw my family running. My aunts and uncles were taking things from the yard and rushing into our house and down to the basement.

My sister took me into the house.

She said, "Don't move. Stay here!"

And I asked, "Why?" but she wouldn't answer me.

The stars looked so beautiful that night and I couldn't get enough of them. I kept going back outside, and she kept taking me back inside and telling me not to move. I wouldn't listen to her. When I went out again, she finally took me into the house and slapped me. She slapped me so hard I can feel the burn to this day. She told me that those weren't stars in the sky, but bullets and rockets flying over our house.

The Taliban had come. They were attacking Herat.

My house was the only one in our extended family that had a basement. It was a small basement, but it provided enough protection for our relatives. After that, whenever any type of attack would happen, everybody would go to our basement immediately. Twenty of us would huddle together and because our bathroom was in the backyard, we had to run outside to a spot near the basement, relieve ourselves, then run back inside.

Not too long after the first attack, my mom woke me up early one morning. It was still dark outside. She told me that we were moving, that we had to leave, and I started crying because I was so attached to the house and to our dog. Traveling with Gorgi would have made us a target for the Taliban, who see dogs as threatening.

We packed up everything in the house and we left Gorgi there. It was very hard for me. The Taliban is a terrorist group, and they were becoming very active in the rural region where I lived. Most of my family left with my dad, and they loaded trucks with our belongings and headed to Kabul, the capital of Afghanistan, where it would be safer. My mom and I were the last ones to leave our house in Herat. I remember hugging Gorgi so long. She didn't know we were leaving for good.

We had to take a very crowded van to get to Kabul. In Afghanistan, there are vans that drive around the country, from province to province, like buses in the United States.

The vans in Afghanistan often have to pass through zones controlled by the Taliban. No one could predict what the Taliban would do when a van would pass through a territory they controlled. Sometimes they would stop the van. Sometimes they would rob the passengers. Sometimes they would do far worse.

We got on the van headed to Kabul, traveling with one of our family friends—a man—for safety. My mom was wearing her burqa. The van rumbled through bumpy landscapes of valleys and isolated hills. I was so tired I fell asleep to the hum of the engine. But then it stopped. I woke up to find the van surrounded by Taliban soldiers.

"Stay close," my mom said. "Stay under my burqa." She was very scared.

The Taliban soldiers ordered everyone off the van. They began searching all of us. I didn't know what they were looking for. They asked my mom a bunch of questions about where we were traveling and whom we were traveling with. We had to pretend that our family friend was my father and that my mother was sick. In the end, they didn't harm us. They let us return to the van.

But when we got to our seats, we saw that there were only a few people who had been allowed back on. There was the driver, two other passengers, and us. The rest of the passengers were still being held by the Taliban.

"Those people are in trouble," my mom said. She told me that they were probably going to be hanged or killed.

We moved into one of the poorest communities in Kabul. If you looked at it from a bird's-eye view, the roads would look like a big maze. The houses were made of mud bricks that had been baked in the sun. Houses were crammed next to each other on both sides of the road.

There was one small stream of water that ran through every street, but it was filled with garbage and sewage. Almost all of the houses had outhouses whose sewage flowed into the streets.

My parents tried to do things differently. In our outhouses, they had dug holes very deep into the ground, so that sewage would not go into the street like our neighbors' toilets did.

When I was around six or seven, my family made me responsible for taking care of the sheep my parents had bought when we arrived in Kabul. That is the typical age for many kids in the country to become a shepherd. Before sunrise, I would wake up and walk more than five miles with our sheep, past the stores and businesses, out of the city, and up to the hills.

Along the way, I would pass the ruins of big buildings and factories that used to provide employment and support our economy. On the hills, the sheep would eat and walk around the ruins of palaces and castles that had been destroyed by the Soviets and the Taliban. Because most of the land was covered with land mines from the Soviet invasion, I had to be very careful and alert at all times to protect myself and the sheep from explosives.

Sometimes I would get into big fights with

some of the shepherd boys. They would shout at me and call me names. This kind of abuse happened for most of my childhood, even at school.

CHAPTER 2

Torment

My school was down the road from where I lived. As in most Afghan schools, the boys were separated from the girls. Girls wore uniforms that covered our bodies, including our wrists and ankles, and that consisted of a naqma, a white head covering, black wide-legged pants, and a black buttoned dress.

I was the youngest in my first-grade class. Many of the other girls who were starting first grade were about eighteen years old.

The United States Agency for International Development, or USAID, gave the school tents that were used as classrooms. Inside were large wooden tables and benches. Teachers would put more people than there should have been on these benches. Sometimes I had to put a leg or my hip on one of the girls sitting next to me, and the girl on the other side of me would have to do the same thing, and we would all just stare at the blackboard.

It wasn't the most educational environment. We looked like a bunch of sheep together. The space was so tight that we couldn't move. We couldn't learn. There would be fifty of us students and only space for about twenty. Everybody would get lice because if one person had them, we'd all get them. We were forced to be so close to each other.

There was always a lot of bribery at the school. Students in my classes would mostly bring money for teachers or the principal. Sometimes a student would promise something that the teachers or the principal needed. If their parents had good jobs, they could use their influence to open up a position for the teacher's family member. Students would bring certain types of rare foods or a computer or a phone. People would even bring sheep as bribes. Animals are treasured in Afghanistan, so bringing someone a sheep was a huge deal.

It's hard to survive with all the poverty in Afghanistan, and the bribes worked. After a payment, the next thing I'd know was that student would either be in a different grade or turn out to be number one in the class. School made me feel like I was nothing because my family was in poverty.

The teachers and other students also treated me terribly because I was Hazara, a minority ethnic group. My mom had always taught me to be very nice to everyone, no matter what ethnic group they were from, no matter if they were rich or poor, abled or disabled. I was always nice to my classmates and shared my snacks with them. Even so, they would steal my books or pencil or whatever they could. None of them wanted to associate with me. No one in Afghanistan associates with Hazaras. It's similar to the caste system in India where people don't associate with outcasts. People believe we are only worthy of being slaves and that we're unintelligent.

Growing up there, I experienced a lot of racism. Nobody wanted to associate with me because I looked Asian and nobody wanted to associate with anyone who looked like me. Because I was the only one in the whole school who had Mongolian features, they'd call me out by saying, "You tight-eye, mice-eating Hazara!" Or they would say, "Ching Chang Chong, go back to China." Maybe they didn't know that Hazaras were in Afghanistan before their people came and conquered everything.

The morning bell started classes, and the afternoon bell signaled the end of school for the day. I always hated when that second bell rang. It was such a nightmare. It was the biggest thing I dreaded at school because that was when the boys would push me around. They would kick and hit me, and the girls would make fun of me. And it wasn't just the students who bullied and abused me.

Teachers would call me up in front of the classroom and hit me with the skinny side of a metal ruler and it would feel like a knife. Or they would put pens between my fingers and squeeze my hand until I screamed or fell down.

Students weren't allowed to wear makeup, but teachers thought I was wearing makeup because my lips are naturally lined and I have very long lashes. They pulled me aside and hit me and told me to get a rag to wipe off the makeup. I kept rubbing my face, trying to prove to them that I had no makeup on, and my skin and lips would bleed.

Teachers would also conduct health checks. We had to put our hands on our desks and they would look at our nails and make sure they were the right length. If they were just a little bit longer than allowed—even a centimeter—they would beat us. This happened to me multiple times because my nails grow so fast.

I'm naturally left-handed, but one teacher said it was haram, forbidden in Islam, to write with my left hand, so she beat me for months until I switched to my right hand. She said only infidels were left-handed.

Despite all this, I would spend hours doing my homework. I would make sure my handwriting was perfect, that everything was perfect, but it didn't matter. My teachers wouldn't even look at my homework.

When I first started school, I would cry to Madar because it hurt so much. I went to school to learn and came home with bruises on my hand that hurt so much I couldn't even carry water buckets to our house, and it was my job to carry water for our family.

My mom went to the principal to complain about my mistreatment, and my principal yelled at her. He cursed at her. He was racist. The principal threatened her by saying, "If you ever come back, I will expel your daughter. Not only that, I will kick you both out on the street because you are nothings."

That was the only school in my community. And in our culture, it's not a norm to speak about one's emotions. You have to keep your feelings inside as a sign of dignity and respect. You're not allowed to be open with anyone. I had no other option but to endure the bullying and abuse.

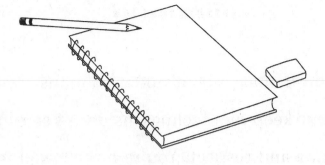

CHAPTER 3

Hope

My older sister found out that there was an organization that wanted to help Afghan children get a Western education at the International School of Kabul (ISK). She was already a student there because another family had helped her apply. My sister told the organization about me and my younger brother, and a staff member contacted us and wanted to make sure we were very serious about learning before allowing us to attend ISK, the only international school in Afghanistan.

The person from the organization asked, "If you are given this opportunity, will you try hard, your best? Will you become the leaders that Afghanistan needs?"

Both my brother and I answered, "Yes! Of course!"

Soon after, thanks to full scholarships we received, we transferred to ISK.

While the public school was down the street from my house, ISK was about five miles away. My brother, sister, and I would walk for over an hour and be exhausted by the time we got there.

We walked between high walls that surrounded homes and created the *sarak*, or street. Some roads were made of cement, but with lots of potholes. Some streets were just soil and rocks. Winters were full of snow and ice. Summers were very hot. Every day, we crossed a small bridge over the Kabul River and took the path alongside it. The river had dried up and was full of trash and sewage. It was also home to a lot of people who were addicts or were homeless. But in the winter, everything around the bridge looked the way I imagined Paris to be. We saw smoke coming out of chimneys and mud houses and little lights around the bridge. It was beautiful! That was the only time you didn't see any pollution in the river. On those winter walks we could feel some escape from assaults and harassment from strangers. In the spring, it was very messy when the snow melted. The road would flood, and we would have to take off our shoes and walk through all the sewage, which smelled absolutely disgusting, but we found the new spring life very beautiful. Planting would begin in the fields we passed on the way, and the fruit trees in the yards we passed by would blossom. On the way, we would judge and praise certain houses. The mud houses were "okay," but not protective enough. The cement houses were nice and our dream homes. Then there were the Pakistani-style "cake houses" which resembled their namesake and even looked like they had fondant icing on them. We liked the design and structure of these houses but not the colors, which always seemed to clash.

The school was about two blocks long, barricaded and blocked off from the rest of the neighborhood. It looked like a military base.

The first day was definitely nerve-racking for me. I remember I was so anxious that my stomach was hurting and I was nauseated. And even now, whenever I am stressed, I get that same pain in my stomach.

We arrived very early in the morning.

Even as nervous as I was, I loved seeing this gleaming, enormous new school. It was like something that I had only seen in a magazine. *Oh my gosh!* I thought. *Am I in America?* I had never seen anything like it!

There was a line of cars near the entrance. Students got out and headed to a common area. My sister, who was three years older, studied in an entirely separate building. She went to her class while my brother and I waited in the courtyard with the other students.

There were so many kids everywhere. Girls weren't wearing a formal uniform, and their hair was curled and in ponytails. Later I learned there was a recess and even toys and balls. I couldn't have imagined a place like this when I was in public school.

It was tough because we didn't know anyone, and we couldn't talk to anyone. My brother and I spoke zero English. The two of us sat down in the courtyard.

At seven-thirty a.m. a bell rang, and all the students stood up, so we stood up, too. Students started forming lines and then teachers came outside and walked up to the lines. My brother and I didn't know who our teachers were or what grade we were in. We had no idea where to go. We were the only two people still not in a line because we didn't know what was happening. We stood in a corner of the common area, feeling nervous and confused, and watched the other kids get in their lines. Some of them laughed and pointed at us. We actually thought we were going to be left there all day and that we would get punished or hit for not going to class.

A staff member finally noticed us and helped us figure out our teachers and grades, and led us to our correct classrooms. My brother and I went to opposite sides of the building because we were in different grades. The first thing I noticed was that not only did this school have chairs, but they actually had one chair per person! I was shocked.

I was trying hard to catch up and learn English, but I had never been exposed to it before. And all I knew was "A, B, C," and "one, two, three," and I wasn't even saying those things right. By the end of the day, I was worn out.

Since English was the primary language at school, the only way I could interact with most of the other students was by playing soccer or participating in activities that didn't require speaking. And that was okay. I was happy I could do that.

After the first week, my brother and I were told that we would be in ELL, but we didn't know what that was. Soon we understood it was a class for students just starting to learn English. Although the ELL teacher, Ms. Shin, didn't speak any Dari—my native tongue—she did an amazing job at teaching us English. While most of her students continued with ELL for the next three years, I became fluent in three months. I never thought I would be able to learn the language that quickly. My brother, who was the type of person who engaged with everyone, became friends with the English-speaking students easily and picked up the language quickly as well, though he had a harder time reading and writing it.

To this day, I appreciate how well Ms. Shin helped me learn English. Her teaching was an important part of how I achieved my goals and received the opportunities I did.

All the teachers at my new school treated me like a human. They saw me as human.

They were kind to me. I was surprised to know that they were there with the intention of really educating students. I was astonished that they didn't punish students when they did something wrong. I went to ISK expecting to get the same punishments I'd always gotten, but there was no abuse at all. Every time I anticipated punishment and it didn't happen, I just thought, *Oh my gosh! What?*

Most of the kids who attended ISK were children of Afghan politicians and governmental leaders, born and raised in the United States. They attended ISK because their parents wanted them to be exposed to their homeland, culture, and their background. They were Westernized and from an upper-class background. None of them were Hazara. They couldn't relate to someone like me who was from Afghanistan, who grew up in poverty, and who was from an ethnic minority.

Still, I befriended several students whose parents had left the United States or another Western country to live in Afghanistan. Whereas some foreigners came for tourism, many expats wanted to invest in the country and make it their permanent home. Because my only close friendships were with foreign students, the tension between me and other Afghan students began to increase. In my culture, associating with foreigners, especially people from the United States, has a very negative connotation. People believe you're allowing yourself to be converted into an American ideologically and religiously. They believe you will become a prostitute or an undesirable person. The Afghan students already didn't accept me for being Hazara and then they started saying, "Yeah, look at her. She's trying to become American."

I had the support of my teachers, but I was still bullied, and it was difficult. Despite it all, I loved my time at ISK. I was a student there from third grade to eighth grade, and I would've attended for longer if the Taliban hadn't put an end to my time there.

CHAPTER 4

Destruction

I heard some of my American teachers talk about growing up and going to libraries. One teacher said there was a library on every corner in America. I asked, "Why don't we have those?" I was always questioning, "Why is it so different here?"

One of my Afghan teachers told me

that there was a time when we had a lot of libraries, and we were as advanced as other countries. She said most of our libraries were destroyed when the Soviets and the Taliban came. She showed me pictures and I saw how beautiful Afghanistan had once been.

Part of me couldn't believe what she was saying and what she was showing me. The truth and reality that I saw in my country was so different from what I saw in those pictures.

Taliban attacks happened every day, probably every hour, in my country. I will never truly understand why there were so many terrorist attacks and why they kept fighting, but I do know it had to do with their thirst for power and their rigid ideology, embedded in their minds as children.

Kabul was the safest place in the country and had plenty of employment opportunities, which was why it held the majority of Afghanistan's population. Unfortunately, terrorist groups like the Taliban must have also realized this, because more and more attacks started to happen in our community. It was terrifying, and it reminded me of when we fled the Taliban's attacks in Herat.

My school had received threats for years. Two years before I attended, the Taliban sent a rocket into the school field and blew up a wall separating the volleyball court from the playground. The Taliban believed that if a school received U.S. funding and Western students attended, it must be corrupting Afghan youth. They believed that girls should never study with boys. They believed that if Afghan or Muslim women were attending those schools, it would corrupt them and turn them into prostitutes or involve them in sex trafficking. The Taliban's harmful and false beliefs contradicted the fact that their own members used women in exactly that way.

One day when I was in sixth grade, we had just come back from lunch, and I was about to open my math book. All of a sudden we heard very loud sounds. At first we thought it was the ongoing construction at the school. It sounded like workers banging on the metal rooftop. But it just kept going and kept going, for thirty minutes. We began to realize that the construction wasn't usually so loud, that the banging didn't happen so fast, so many times in a row.

Then we heard sirens and alarms. Cage doors on our classrooms came clanging down. We went on full lockdown mode. We couldn't contact our parents. Teachers radioed one another and instructed us to be quiet.

Our classroom was closest to where the

Taliban had taken position. We had to keep low on the floor and away from the windows. Students cried, and the teachers tried so hard to keep us quiet, but we were freaked out. Teachers kept repeating, "Calm down. Calm down. Please calm down." They tried to give us books to read to distract us. They said, "Whatever you do, you must remain quiet."

This went on for hours.

By the time we were finally able to leave school, it was pitch-black outside. It was around ten p.m., but the fight was still going on.

Other students' families had cars and lived nearby, but my sister, brother, and I had to walk for miles back home. Teachers showed us an unfamiliar path out of the school. Still, we had to be extra cautious. As we walked, we tried to keep hidden in the dark, sneaking behind buildings and trees until we made it home.

In the middle of my eighth-grade year, a bomb blew up my street at six o'clock in the morning. I had been sleeping when the explosion picked me up and slammed me into a wall. I blacked out, and when I came back to consciousness I had no idea what was happening. Everything around me was still dark and spinning. Windows were shattered.

My mom had just left for her job cleaning houses, and I called her. She couldn't get in touch until the next day. The blast had broken her phone. The bridge near our house was wrecked and she was stuck on the other side of it.

A week after that explosion, the school called and told us to stay home. They said they would send homework for us to complete but that we shouldn't come in. A few weeks later, they checked in and said students could return to school in a few more weeks. A few more weeks came and went, and we continued to stay home. Then they announced that it was winter break and that afterward students could return to school.

But that didn't happen, either. Finally, in the summer, they told us that they were shutting down the school completely. There were too many security threats, and the school could not remain open.

CHAPTER 5

Legacy

In Afghanistan, men are supposed to be the head of the household. They are expected to protect and provide for their family. Men are never supposed to be sick or be weak.

My dad couldn't protect us or provide for us because, for most of my life, my dad was ill.

I don't have memories of my dad being well. I don't have memories of him not needing our help. When I was growing up, there were many times when he wouldn't be able to feed himself or talk or use the bathroom. We had to feed him and wash him and bathe him.

When I was around eight years old and when my dad was feeling well enough, he would tell me stories after lunch in the living room as he sat on a *toshak*, a long wool-stuffed cushion, and drank *doogh*, a liquidy yogurt. My dad might have realized that he had never shared much with me and that he was getting older and there wasn't much more time for me to know and to understand what had happened in his life.

Even when he told me about being kidnapped, I didn't understand the connection to my dad being paralyzed. The Taliban kidnapped my father three times, and he managed to escape twice. The third time the Taliban kidnapped my father, they tortured him in front of my mom. They tortured him to the point that he was barely alive.

As an eight-year-old, I would hear these stories, and I would think, *Yeah, but you're a man; you can't be sick because of that!* I believed that nothing could ever be wrong with a man.

I lived around many elderly people who were sick most of the time, so I believed my dad was just sick because he was old. It wasn't until middle school that I started to understand why he was paralyzed, and it took me a long time to process what had happened to him.

My father was full of so many stories, and I learned that he was very adventurous as a young man. I would listen intently and at times would become so excited, picturing people and places in my head. "Well, wait!" I'd say, jumping in to ask a question or for details.

These were stories of courage, resilience, independence, and taking risks. In them, my father was always the one standing out, pushing back against what was "normal" and deemed appropriate by society. I valued the themes and lessons of each story, and I clearly remember the story he told about when he was first captured by the Taliban.

As a teenager, he ran away from home and started to work with a foreign organization that helped the poor around the country. The organization traveled to different towns, staying at guest houses they owned. During these trips, my dad would be the *chowkidar*, the person who guarded the door, protecting others from danger.

During one of his missions in Herat, the Taliban found out that foreigners were staying in the guest houses and started to launch attacks. These attacks usually started with grenades blowing up the entrance to the building, followed by shooting into the house and setting a fire to destroy it. My dad was the guard one night when an attack began. They set the guest house on fire, burning it down, and broke into other houses. They shot the people inside. My dad was there, helping people escape. Most of them were women.

Because he put their lives ahead of his own, my dad was still in the guest house when members of the Taliban broke in. They pointed a gun at people from the organization, and my dad immediately put himself in the line of fire. He stood between the

Taliban and the foreigners. He was ready to take a bullet for them, but the Taliban didn't shoot. Instead, they kidnapped and tortured him. They beat him with the butt of a gun and knocked out all of his teeth to where only the roots remained in his jaw. He eventually escaped.

I saw that my father had been brave and selfless. He was pure courage. His stories instilled in me the importance of being a fighter, a risk- taker. His experiences gave me wings of courage.

Because of the violence against Hazaras, I began to question our history. I wondered if people were taking revenge on us now because of something that we had done ages ago. In school, throughout every grade, history books never mentioned anything positive about the Hazaras. Every single history book talked about Tajik and Pashtun achievements, but there was hardly any information about Hazaras, and the small amount of information there was focused on how we had always been slaves, plantation workers, and the lowest of the low in Afghan society.

I couldn't research Hazara history because I didn't have any access to the internet, and libraries had been destroyed by the Taliban. I turned to people who were elderly and held more knowledge about our history.

They ended up being my greatest resource. These elders told me how they had faced persecution, how their parents and their grandparents had faced this treatment. Because of their stories, I stopped questioning whether we had done something in the past to deserve such cruelty. Hazaras had been persecuted for centuries, since the 1800s.

Elders would tell me how civilization was much better before the Pashtun dynasty took over Afghanistan, that there were many ethnic groups and people got along in those days. The Pashtun dynasty took over everything. They wanted to conquer the land, start their own civilization, and put their policies into practice. They did exactly that. When I learned this history, what went through my head was the children's movie *The Prince of Egypt*. All I could picture was how all those people were enslaved and how the Pharaoh beat them.

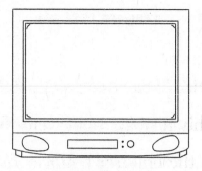

CHAPTER 6

Bloodshed

In the late seventies and early eighties, when the Soviets were in Afghanistan, a group of militia men banded together to overthrow the Taliban and the Soviets. Ahmad Shah Massoud, one of the leaders, was Tajik, one of the ethnic majorities. When I was in the fourth grade, Tajiks were celebrating the anniversary of Massoud's death, calling him a martyr. To honor him, they started shooting Hazaras in public, in the open bazaar, with their guns and armed trucks.

The killings happened over an entire month.

Around this same time the Pashtuns, another ethnic group that is a major persecutor of Hazaras, started taking over our land, mostly in large Hazara communities. The largest takeover happened in Bamyan, a province that is predominantly Hazara.

During this time, it was chaos. Hazara towns completely vanished. Big groups of Pashtun men entered Hazara communities late at night. They took away all of the people's possessions, their sheep, their weapons. They took their belongings, and then they took families far away from their homes, to the mountainsides. They blindfolded them and killed them.

Many were beheaded and slaughtered.

They dumped the bodies on mountainsides, hillsides, ditches, and even on the roadsides—and these were roads that people regularly used for travel. You would be driving along, and there would be bodies on the sides of the road.

Everyone could see it.

When the killings first started, I had just gotten home from school and immediately started watching the evening news with my parents. It was on every channel.

My parents discussed the news, and when the news mentioned specific towns, my parents would say, "This many people from this town got killed, and they're gone. Their whole families. They are gone." They'd wondered about who they knew who might have been murdered. They'd ask, "What if it's this person or that person?"

We stopped visiting relatives because it was too dangerous to travel. My parents were frightened our neighborhood would be next, and most of the Hazaras in our community warned us, "The Pashtuns have been sending out threats. They are trying to attack every Hazara community that they come in contact with." They cautioned us not to be out in the streets or in public past a certain time.

I was always alert, anticipating an attack. I would walk to school, always afraid, hyper-vigilant. At school, the kids, who were mostly Pashtuns and Tajiks, would make fun of me. Then they would say, "It's surprising that we haven't gotten you yet."

I thought that our neighborhood would be next because of how many Hazara commu-nities had been attacked and how they had been slaughtered so mercilessly, and yet the government wasn't doing anything. All they did was hold a mass burial, say something like, *Oh, we're sorry for these people*, and then carry on with their day.

The majority of the government was led by Pashtuns or Tajiks. They were running the entire country and were in charge of everything. Government leaders focused on what benefited them and their own ethnic groups. They were okay with policies that discriminated against others, and that could even eliminate a whole group of people. They didn't believe that all groups were as deserving of life and happiness as their own. Even now, there are very few Hazaras in the parliament.

As the slaughtering continued, the media kept displaying the awful footage of people being killed. The worst part was that some of the footage that was being shown was filmed by the people who had committed these crimes. The media accepted their footage because, like the government, media organizations were run by the Tajiks and Pashtuns. They also knew viewers would tune in to watch these horrific videos. The murderers filmed their acts because they wanted everyone to know how powerful they were and what they were capable of doing. They wanted everyone to know that they were fearless, that they would go as far as they needed to go to make their race pure. The video footage served as a warning. They wanted every Hazara to believe their community was next.

Many of the Hazaras I knew started to disassociate themselves from their counterparts to escape persecution. They started saying that they were not Hazara, that they just looked like it. If their names sounded Hazara, they changed them.

I was losing so much of my culture that it started to affect my mental health, as it does to so many people. Whenever I would see a mass killing on the news, it would kill a part of me, too. It would make me so depressed that

I'd start to cry. My throat would hurt from seeing and hearing it all the time.

I kept it inside me for so long because I was surrounded by so much opposition. I was surrounded by people who were letting these things happen. I didn't know how to advocate for my people. I didn't know how to raise my voice. All I knew was that I was hurting for so long.

CHAPTER 7

Fear

When I started seventh grade, my family was living in a house close to the Kabul River, which was full of sewage. It flooded all the time. We lived in a very impoverished area, and our family, once again, was one of the very few Hazaras that lived nearby. My mom started walking with us to and from school.

I didn't know it at the time, but she did this because she was receiving death threats over the phone and was concerned for our safety. She also started asking me and my sister to wear clothes that covered us up a bit more and to consider wearing a hijab. I became frustrated and argued with her, saying things like, "You never back down," and "Why are you changing your ideology all of a sudden?"

I was both angry and hurt. I didn't understand what was happening to my mom. I was also becoming a teenager, so I was more emotional than I used to be.

One day after school, I was waiting to walk home with my siblings and my mom when my older sister said to me, "We're not going home."

"What the heck are you talking about?" I asked. "Of course we're going home."

Something bad had happened. My mom didn't want us home because it was too dangerous. But my sister didn't tell me that.

She said, "We're just going to stay at somebody else's place."

We ended up staying at a family friend's house near our school, and later that night my mom called us. She explained that after she dropped us off at school that morning, she had been walking home and several men ran her over with a motorcycle. These were the same men that had been threatening her over the phone. She told us they had harassed and assaulted her a few times before. Finally she opened up to us, but only because the death threats were escalating.

She told me, "You need to stay away from the house for the next three weeks."

We stayed with our friend, but we didn't have any change of clothes and wore the same outfits for almost a month. As the weeks went by, my dad's health worsened, and my mom feared we might lose him.

"Can we please see him in case something happens to him?" we asked over and over, but my mom said that it wasn't safe for us to come near the house.

She said, "Every time I step outside, I see the same men who ran me over." My mother was on lockdown and hadn't even been able to go out to buy food for weeks.

At the end of the three weeks, we devised a plan to grab a change of clothes and to see our father. His condition was worsening, especially because it was too unsafe for him to leave the house and go to a doctor.

We woke up around one or two a.m. and changed into hoodies and dark clothes our friend lent us. We tried to disguise ourselves to look like boys. We left our friend's house and met my mom at the bridge over the Kabul River near our house.

My mom wore her burqa that she hadn't

put on since the Taliban had come to the country. Her burqa still had holes from the time the Taliban were shooting at her and her friends in 1994. She took us into the house, and we saw our father. We got new sets of clothes, and we left that same night. Talk about being refugees in your own home.

My mom started to wear her burqa whenever she went out in public. She didn't want to be recognized. She said we could come back home and that we needed to start wearing hijabs to be safe. *Okay, fine.* I thought. *I guess that's what we're going to do.*

But we still weren't safe. My mom said that she would see the threatening men constantly, that they were following us. They were waiting for us outside of school, by the grocery store near our house, when we went to the bazaar, everywhere. They started throwing letters with death threats into our yard. This went on for a couple years, before my school told us it was shutting down permanently.

Around this time, our family received some good news. My sister had applied to a U.S. boarding school and was accepted. When she received her student visa, she left immediately. Then it was just my parents, my younger brother, and me, which meant that I had to be the breadwinner of the family.

I started tutoring, teaching children English, but the job didn't make enough money to support us. My mom tried to sneak out of the house so she could find homes that needed cleaning, and she would spend hours and hours cleaning homes. She would make two dollars in two weeks from her work. I thought it was just ridiculous. But we had to do it.

We were overwhelmed by the death threats and fear and trying to survive, and things seemed only to worsen.

CHAPTER 8

Escape

At night, we took turns staying awake and keeping guard over our house. We looked out the window and kept watch. Our house wasn't secure, and the structure wasn't strong. It was easy to enter the yard, and the front door wasn't stable. It probably would have fallen down with one strong kick. I was afraid.

Every night people would climb on the roof, and we weren't sure what exactly they were doing or if we needed to protect ourselves. I think the only reason they didn't break into our house was because we had dogs. Any time a stranger was close to the house, the dogs would alert us by barking and growling.

I didn't realize that the reason I always felt sick might be because of the death threats, the Taliban attacks, the school closure. I had a long conversation with my mom. I told her that I couldn't imagine this being the end of my educational journey. I told her that I had a much bigger vision for myself than what was happening in our lives. I wanted something more.

We knew it was extremely dangerous for us to leave those four walls and our yard, but we made a plan together. The two of us would brace ourselves and walk out the door and go to the internet café. I wanted to apply to schools outside the country.

Even as I completed applications at the internet café, I felt hopeless. *Nobody's going to accept me*, I thought. *Why would they want me? I didn't even finish my eighth-grade year and I'm from Afghanistan.* But I applied anyway.

The death threats worsened to the point where my mom received a phone call from a shopkeeper nearby. He told her there were men with axes and machetes asking for our names, asking where our home was, and when we would be there.

He said, "I don't know what's going on. But it doesn't look like a good situation, so I would tell you guys to not come around. And I'll give you a call when these guys are gone."

My tutoring job had been supporting the family, but it was too dangerous to work, with men circling our house each night, intending to harm us. They poisoned our dogs, and then they tried to break in several times. We managed to hide when they did, or our cries for help would bring our neighbors out into the street to scare them off.

We knew we had to flee. Within a week, we sold our possessions and got our visas to move to India.

My family was in India for a few months. I was unable to go to school. My family hardly had money to buy even one meal a day. We had no pillows or carpets, and we slept on hard floors. We shared two cups to drink from, and spent most days trying to survive in the heat. The temperature and humidity were so high that people would routinely pass out from the heat.

My father became even more ill. We feared our time there might be his last days. On top of his health crisis, my mother also became severely ill. She had sores all over her body, and her limbs had swollen to triple the size they normally were. She couldn't even put on her shoes. This made me fear for her life as well. I was beginning to think that I might lose both of my parents.

While in India, I heard back from a boarding school in the United States and they told me

I was accepted with a full scholarship. They assumed I was still in a position where I could pick up and leave at any time, but I told them that wasn't the case anymore.

I replied, "I'm so grateful to be accepted. But I can no longer attend your school because of my family situation." If I left, my mom, my dad, and my brother would die of starvation. My parents were unemployed in a new country and unable to speak the language. My family was completely dependent on me.

The school continued to check in on me and repeated that they would love for me to attend.

One evening, I broke down and cried to

my mom and told her about the situation. "I just want to bring change, so that families like us don't ever have to go through this ever again."

She sat down and started to cry. She said, "Your dad and I have lived our lives. Whatever happens to us, happens to us, and that is fine because we've already lived our lives."

She said, "Everything we sacrificed, we sacrificed for our children, so they can reach their dreams and bring change to our country." She was giving me her blessing to leave. This was the biggest decision of my lifetime, and it was very difficult to know what to do.

I spent a month thinking about my

choices. Finally, I accepted the U.S. school's offer. My mom had said that my siblings and I were the future. She believed the change that was needed was in our hands. She told me to go.

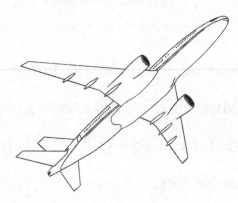

Epilogue

Leaving my mom and dad in India was one of the hardest goodbyes imaginable.

When I got off the plane at the crowded airport in Washington, D.C., people were staring at me. I think they were looking at me because I wore glasses that were very badly broken. I still had to wear them because my vision was so bad, and my family couldn't afford new ones. I think maybe people were worried that I was a victim of physical abuse or sex trafficking.

Before I could leave the airport, security pulled me aside. They fingerprinted me multiple times and instructed me to answer questions on official forms and sign many documents. I had to state that I did not arrive with an intent to cause harm to the U.S. government. I felt intimidated, overwhelmed, and scared by them and the hours-long process. But then I finally got past airport security. Donors who had covered my flight to the United States drove me across the country, where I finally met my Texan host family, the Moores, and they were really nice and sweet. They took me out to eat and showed me my room in their house, which they'd furnished with a new bed and new blanket just for me. During my time with them, the Moores introduced me to a lot of foods that were new to me, and they supported me financially, including helping me travel.

My new high school was an elite school in Bullard, a rural town in Texas. It was so big that students walked from building to building, crossing streets to get to their next class, similar to a college campus. The school had a huge auditorium, a football field, a soccer field, and a museum that was widely known in the area.

As I started to become more familiar with the culture, I wore my first dress without pants underneath, which was a big deal to me, even though I still had a hard time showing my arms. In my PE class, I started to wear the mandatory uniform of shorts and a shirt and thought, *Oh my gosh, this is nice*, because it was so hot in Texas. I started to love buying clothes with my host mom and exploring fashion. I even had cowboy boots. When I made it to the homecoming court, she helped me try on multiple dresses until we finally found the right one.

But I was mentally stuck back at home, watching the news constantly and always hurting for all the lives lost. Given the opportunities that I had, I started to advocate for the people who were suffering in my country by speaking publicly at school and local events. Soon organizations and schools reached out to me and invited me to speak in their states or at their events.

At first I spoke about issues like women's rights, and breaking stereotypes about Afghanistan, but more recently I've been speaking about the Hazara genocide. Sometimes I feel like I started this advocacy journey a little too late, and I feel guilty. This year alone, I have spent so much time and energy focusing on this issue, because hundreds of people are dying every day from my ethnic group, just like the Rwandan genocide, and people only seem to be aware of the U.S. war against terror in Afghanistan.

But every group that faces persecution or oppression is valuable and deserves people's care and attention. One person's life is not more important than another's, no matter their ethnicity or color or class.

A life is a life.

Soon after I started school in the United States my dad passed away, and I lost communication with my mom. I now only have contact with her a couple of times per year as she struggles with financial insecurity and limited access to the internet.

A couple months into my arrival, my best friends' house was attacked by the Taliban. They blew up their family's strong, tall, metal gate with grenades and detonated a bomb after shooting my two friends and their father. I will never forget the moment sitting at my computer, sobbing in shock as I watched the house that I had made so many memories in burning and saw my friends' coffins.

I lost so many friends and family, people who had all these hopes and dreams, who were working hard to make our country a better place, to make this world a better place, and their efforts were cut short.

I keep fighting a little bit of their fight, because that's the best that I can do for them. And, at this point, I don't have anything more to fear. If you want to make the world a place where justice and freedom are more valued than racism, persecution, and oppression, it's up to you. You have to take hard risks and it won't be an easy journey.

But if you stay silent, revolution and change will never happen.

And if you wait to speak, it may be too late.

Continue the Discussion

What is the Taliban?

The Taliban is a political and religious group, known for their strict adherence to Islamic laws and support of terrorism. After a long Afghan civil war that lasted over a decade, the Taliban rose to power in 1996.

While the Taliban were in power, women and girls were not allowed to attend school or work, and they could not leave the house without a male guardian. Punishments for not adhering to these laws were violent and cruel, sometimes resulting in death. Additionally, they allowed terrorists to live in the country and run training camps.

The Taliban were removed from power in 2001. They returned to power in 2021, just before the planned withdrawal of U.S. military forces.

Is the Taliban still considered a threat in Afghanistan?

Although the Taliban hadn't been in power since 2001, in 2021, President Biden announced that the United States would withdraw troops from Afghanistan before September 11 of that year. Before that deadline, in late August, the Taliban took control again, creating an extremely dangerous situation for all civilians— especially Hazaras. Thousands of Afghan people tried to escape in the last days of August, leading to violence and chaos at the Kabul airport and a deadly bombing carried out by another terrorist group, ISIS-K.

How long have Hazaras faced persecution and violence?

Before the nineteenth century, Hazaras were the largest ethnic group, and now they comprise approximately 9 percent of the population. In 1893, more than half of the Hazara population were massacred or displaced, and since then they continue to face persecution. When the Taliban were in power, violence against them increased and thousands were murdered and fled their homes during mass killings.

In Afghanistan, discrimination against Hazaras continues to this day. In Pakistan, they are considered the most persecuted ethnic minority. According to human rights organizations, hundreds of Hazaras have been murdered and thousands injured in recent years.

What advocacy is Freshta doing these days?

Freshta publicly speaks about the persecution of Hazaras in various settings, including universities, events, and podcasts. She co-founded Hazara Advocates USA, whose members work to raise awareness of the issues her family faced and call on legislators to support U.S. aid for Afghanistan.

At the start of the pandemic, she began sewing masks for the homeless to protect their well-being. Her efforts have grown into Sew True Products, a small business that donates proceeds to various efforts, including tuition for Afghan students.

In addition to activism, what else is Freshta up to?

Because she witnessed cruel and unlawful acts throughout her life, Freshta is passionate about transforming the legal system. She is pursuing an education in pre-law and international relations at Calvin University and hopes to intern at the United Nations and the American Enterprise Institute. Additionally, she is the financial provider for her three nieces and nephew in Kabul, who are young leaders in Afghanistan.

Engagement guide available.

Find out more at

wwnorton.com/i-witness-series

Get Involved

1. Stay informed.

Do research and interact with people of all different backgrounds. Remain teachable: this allows you to know the facts instead of affirming stereotypes and misconceptions. Seek out reputable news sources and firsthand accounts, which allow you to see these issues through the eyes of people directly involved. There will always be the internet and textbooks, but primary sources will always teach you something more eye-opening.

2. Speak out.

Call your lawmakers about redirecting aid sent to Afghanistan. If the United States continues to aid Afghanistan with our tax dollars, it is important that the aid is given to those invested in developing and supporting the country, and not in carrying out the Hazara genocide.

3. Support.

Donate, share, participate, volunteer, or help with campaigns. No matter where you are, you are invited to participate in the mission of Sew True and Hazara Advocates USA. You can follow these organizations online to learn more.

Timeline

1994

The Taliban rises to power in Afghanistan, making promises of peace and strict adherence to Islamic laws.

1998

May 8: The Taliban carries out mass murders of Hazaras in Mazar-e Sharif, killing between two thousand and five thousand people.

2000

May: The Taliban mass-murder Hazaras near Baghlan and Samangan Provinces.

2001

Freshta moves from Herat to Kabul, traveling with her mother in a van.

January 8–11: The Taliban kidnap and kill 150 Hazaras in the Yakaolang District.

October 7: U.S. and British military forces launch air strikes and bomb Taliban targets.

November 13: The Taliban flee Kabul after battling with the Northern Alliance, a military group formed to overthrow them.

December 7–9: The Taliban leave Kandahar and surrender Zabul, one of the final places they occupied. Many consider this the end of the Taliban regime.

2002

June 2002: Hamid Karzai is picked to lead Afghanistan as the country transitions to a new government.

2003

Freshta begins to shepherd near Kabul.

Freshta attends an Afghan public school in Kabul where she is bullied and abused for being Hazara.

2004

January: Afghan delegates approve a new constitution that includes a democratic presidential system, elections, and a national assembly.

2006

Violence resurges and the number of suicide bombings sharply rises. The Taliban claim responsibility for many of these attacks.

2008

Freshta stops shepherding and begins to attend the International School of Kabul (ISK).

Mass killings of Hazaras occur throughout Afghanistan, in provinces including Bamyan.

2010

ISK suffers an attack by the Taliban while school is in session, and it continues late into the night.

2012

May: ISK closes permanently because of security threats.

Freshta and her family receive constant death threats and flee to India.

2013

Freshta decides to attend a U.S. boarding school and leaves India.

2021

April 13: President Joe Biden announces that all U.S. troops will exit Afghanistan before September 11, 2021.

August 16: Quickly and violently, the Taliban again take control of the country, leaving thousands in peril. Many rush to flee before the August 31 deadline that President Biden set as the final day U.S. troops would be in the country.

Author's Acknowledgments

I would like to give huge thanks to Instagram for running ads for the International Congress of Youth Voices in my feed. I cannot express enough how life-changing getting to be part of this movement has been. Special thanks to Amanda Uhle, Dave Eggers, Zainab Nasrati, and Zoë Ruiz for always helping me reach different heights and pursue different opportunities. More importantly, thank you very much for seeing my story as worthy of sharing, and for seeing me as worthy of sharing my story.

Agha Jan and Madar Jan, thank you for risking your lives every day for me to have a successful future. Thank you for the numerous sacrifices that forever shaped how I treat others, how I view the world, and how I appreciate the small and great things. You taught me how to be fierce, resilient, and a justice warrior. If it weren't for you, I would not be here today, not because you gave me life, but because of the number of times you willingly laid down your lives so that I would see another day. The lessons you taught me will forever remain with me.

I would like to give huge thanks to Mr. Scott Dwyer for all of his time spent on getting this book started. He devoted a tremendous number of hours, in and out of office, over the weekends even, to make sure I understood what this process would look like and mean for me. Thank you for your much appreciated time to help me understand every detail and take on this project with confidence. Thank you for so willingly taking such an important role in part of my life. More importantly, thank you for inspiring me to pursue a career in law and serve others with kindness and understanding.

Ma and Poppy, thank you for teaching me what it is like to finally be a kid. You filled up the empty, missing part of my heart in so many ways. Thank you for letting me say the words *mom* and *dad* again. You have been the perfect examples of love, success, and motivation, and what I want to be when I grow up :) Thank you for teaching me lessons that have made significant impacts in my life.

TJ, you inspire me to keep fighting every day. Your experiences and stories have shaped me in ways that you may not be aware of, but I am so blessed to call you brother. Thank you for believing in me, encouraging me, and reminding me what being fierce looks like. I am so thankful life reunited us on a different side of the world.

Tabasum, I could go on forever about the miracle you have been in so many lives. From the moment I held you in my arms, I felt the most calm peace, I felt fire and light all over you. Leaving you was one of the hardest goodbyes, but every day you remind me to fight for education, for your generation, for peace and security so that not one more child grows up to think a graveyard is their playground. You have taught me to stay committed, work hard, and remain teachable.

Hamid, Beheshta, and Marwa, you are the youngest leaders I already see making great changes in the world. Thank you for teaching me to smile, to be thankful, and to have childlike faith. Thank you for allowing me to take an important role in your life and support your education journey.

Rode and JP, you were some of the most wonderful friends I will ever know. I have mourned you being gone from Earth for years, but thinking of our memories keeps me hopeful. I miss you, and at every graduation I complete, I always think of you and will continue to live and serve in memory of your brave hearts.

Tim, you have been one of the biggest support systems I have ever had. I have no words to express what a blessing you have been to me. You never fail to encourage me to overcome my fears and are always willing to help me take the next big steps in life. Thank you for helping me invest in Tabasum, Hamid, Beheshta, and Marwa's lives. You have been a light, my partner in crime, and my sunshine during storms.

I also thank Jan Schuitema and everyone who took in a complete stranger under their roof, provided them shelter and food. You will always hold a special place in my heart. You blessed me in so many ways and I hope to serve just like you for the rest of my life.

This list does not do justice in expressing my gratitude to every single soul who has impacted my life. For every single person always so interested to participate in Hazara Advocates USA, thank you. Thank you for contributing your platform to expand awareness about the Hazara genocide and volunteering on campaigns. To the hundreds of you who helped me to serve the homeless population in the city of Grand Rapids when the pandemic shut down shelters, thank you so much for your outpouring love. Because of your help, Sew True now is able to provide assistance to not only our homeless brothers and sisters, but various communities. To everyone who has always extended a helping hand, a word of encouragement, the most delicious banana bread, and free service on my car (Mr. and Mrs. VanBeek) to help me get from conferences to the airport and back and forth. To the many who funded my projects, conferences, and campaigns, found me worthy of partaking in their events, please know you have made a lasting impact.

Editors' Acknowledgments

The editors would like to extend special thanks to the Young Editors Project (YEP), which connects young readers to manuscripts in progress. The program gives meaningful opportunities for young people to be part of the professional publishing process and gives authors and publishers meaningful insights into their work. Special thanks to Anika Hussain; Jennifer Kahlenberg's sixth-grade class in Northfield, Illinois; Orla, Harrison, Amaya, Elena, Noah, Emi, William, Morgan, Romilly, Lydia, Jasmine, Lily, Holly, Ruby, Otis,

EDITORS' ACKNOWLEDGMENTS

Elana, Maxime, Archie, and Ava from the United Kingdom; Ilaria from Trieste, Italy; and Eileen and Corinne from New York City.

www.youngeditorsproject.org

About I, Witness

I, Witness is a nonfiction book series that tells important stories of real young people who have faced and conquered extraordinary contemporary challenges. There's no better way for young readers to learn about the world's issues and upheavals than through the eyes of young people who have lived through these times.

Proceeds from this book series support the work of the International Alliance of Youth Writing Centers and its sixty-plus member organizations. These nonprofit writing centers are joined in a common belief that young people need places where they can write and be heard, where they can have their voices celebrated and amplified.

www.youthwriting.org